Dolls for Sale

By the same author

STORYBOOK DOLLS

Dolls for Sale

Valerie Janitch
with photographs by Rob Matheson

FABER & FABER   LONDON & BOSTON

First published in 1980
by Faber and Faber Limited
3 Queen Square London WC1N 3AU
Printed and bound in Great Britain by
Fakenham Press Limited, Fakenham, Norfolk.
All rights reserved

Conditions of Sale
This book is sold subject to the condition that it
shall not, by way of trade or otherwise, be lent,
re-sold, hired out or otherwise circulated without
the publisher's prior consent in any form of bind-
ing or cover other than that in which it is pub-
lished and without a similar condition including
this condition being imposed on the subsequent
purchaser.

British Library Cataloguing in Publication Data

Janitch, Valerie
    Dolls for sale
    1. Dollmaking
    2. Soft toy making
    I. Title
    745.59'22   TT175

ISBN 0–571–11535–7
ISBN 0–571–11536–5 Pbk

Contents

———◆◆◆◆◆———

Colour Plates

———◄•••►———

Market Research and Gentle Persuasion

The secret of successful selling

———◆••••◆———

What makes someone buy a doll? Obviously it depends on the type of person, and the type of doll. A small boy will pick a grinning cowboy complete with lasso, while his grandmother chooses a frilly-bonneted baby in a lacy cradle. So it makes sense to think hard about your potential buyers and plan your dolls with maximum appeal to *them*.

When your customers are mainly parents, relatives or friends buying presents for small children, it's usually best to play safe with traditional rag dolls. These should be soft, cuddly, wide-eyed and smiling happily: but strongly-made, hygienic and safety-minded, to satisfy the most practical mother. A totally different kind of doll will probably be popular with teenagers. Youngsters tend to be impulse-buyers: they may not be short of money, but dolls need to be extrovert and gimmicky—a fun decoration for bedroom or den. Research may be necessary to hit on the right mix of subject and treatment: an 'old-fashioned girl' might prove to be a best-seller, but the secret of her success will probably be your very modern approach!

Having decided on the market you are aiming to conquer, a little self-examination will help to formulate your sales technique. So I have compiled a set of practical guidelines: follow these and you can be confident your work will have all the advantages of a thoroughly professional approach.

Practical Guidelines

Your count-down to profitable doll-making

———◆•••◆———

Time is Money is the never-to-be-forgotten Golden Rule: the less time you spend on each doll, the higher your output ... so the greater your profit. Begin by studying your market and decide the type of doll which will have the greatest appeal.

Choose subjects which are reasonably quick to make: avoid complicated designs with too much time-consuming detail.

Small is sensible: large, floppy dolls take up too much space on a crowded stall or counter and don't look their best, either. Smaller dolls are easier to sell: they are quicker and cheaper to make, more convenient to package and display, and the dolls' endearing size usually increases their charm.

Inexpensive materials will increase your profit margin—but do make sure the quality is good: poor materials create untold problems, so they're a false economy.

'Hand-made' is something to be proud of. Exploit it; emphasise that special charm that manufactured dolls usually lack.

Try to give your dolls an individual touch, either in the design or in the packaging: perhaps an attractive label or tag displaying your name—and that of the doll, too.

Mass-production means increased production: half-a-dozen at a time is a lot quicker than making six individual dolls.

Look out for helpful short cuts: a tube of fabric adhesive is just one incredible time-saver. Ready-embroidered trimmings are another.

Attractive packaging is practical and helps to sell.

Cheap is not always cheerful: it could be worth spending a little more on an attractive trimming—if it turns an ordinary doll into an exclusive model for which you can charge considerably more.

It pays to adopt a professional approach: high standards are reflected in the finished product. Customers should buy your work *because they want the doll,* not as a generous contribution to the church steeple fund or, worse still, as an act of kindness to you!

Plan ahead. Working out a plan of campaign before you begin is the only way to avoid mistakes and ensure a profit. It's worth sitting down beforehand, with a sheet of paper, to plan the venture in a business-like way.

Pricing the finished product

It is wise to try to calculate a rough estimated price before you begin: then you will know what profit margin you can expect. Have a look at the competition, if you can, and base your reckoning on similar dolls in shops and stores.

Cost out your projected doll, not forgetting any hidden extras like telephone calls, postage or travel to locate and obtain materials, and delivery. Add in every scrap of ribbon and length of elastic: they mount up alarmingly when you're making six at a time. Check your arithmetic and then decide an asking price. Remember, the price the customer pays is not clear profit: you must first deduct the cost of materials and your expenses.

Rosebud, Nanook and Papoose

Millie and Edward

Some General Notes

———◆••••◆———

Measurements

Both Imperial and metric measures are given in every instance. Use one or the other, but *don't* compare the two. If you do, you will find they differ. To avoid eye-strain counting tiny fractions or millimetres, I have always given the nearest practical measurement, rather than an accurate conversion. So just use the ruler you prefer: as long as you make a doll all-metric or all-Imperial, you can be sure the result will be perfectly in proportion.

When the *direction of measurements* is not specifically stated, the depth is always given first, followed by the width: i.e. 5 × 10 cm (2 × 4 in) = 5 cm (2 in) deep × 10 cm (4 in) wide.

Making Patterns

TRACING PATTERNS: Use household greaseproof paper or good quality white tissue paper, and a sharp pencil. When a fold is indicated, always *fold the paper*: run your thumbnail along to sharpen the crease, then place it exactly level with the fold-line on the pattern. Trace through the double thickness and then cut out, holding tightly or pinning to ensure the paper stays exactly together as you cut. Open out the pattern, so that you can cut your fabric flat.

SCALE PATTERNS: Use graph paper, or draw the diagrams to the correct scale on tracing paper (as above) fixed firmly over a sheet of graph or squared paper. Use a sharp pencil and ruler, and compasses.

CUTTING SMALL CIRCLES (FOR EYES, ETC): To mark accurate circles on felt, find a cap from a pen or toothpaste tube, a tiny bottle top, a thimble—or any similar round object with a firm rim—the same size as the required circle. Rub a white or light-coloured wax crayon or chalk all round the rim, then press it down firmly on your felt—and twist, taking care not to move the position. This will leave a clear impression on the felt: cut carefully round the marked line with small, sharp scissors.

17

Sweet and Simple

Cradle-babes for the nursery

Just the baby alone would make an attractive sales item—but nestling in a padded carrying cradle, its charm is doubled. Both baby and basket are simple, quick and economical to make.

This first example demonstrates the theme of the whole book. One basic design is interpreted in numerous ways to produce a variety of surprisingly individual dolls, resulting in an eye-catching and amusing display. Three babies are described here: the picture on the cover of this book shows how just minor variations in colour and trimming can inspire a whole nursery of little ones.

Rosebud, the basic doll

MATERIALS: A 5 cm (2 in) diameter circle of flesh-coloured felt for the face
Felt for hood and body (see figs 2 and 3)
A scrap of brown, blue or alternative felt for eyes
Medium or light-weight knitting wool or yarn, or furnishing fringe, for hair
Kapok or Polyester fiberfill for stuffing
Lace, braid, embroidery, lambswool or alternative, and ribbon (optional), to trim hood and bag (see illustrations)
Black sewing thread for features
2 black sequins for eyes
All-purpose fabric adhesive

Cut the face, hood and body once each in appropriate felts (or fabric).

HEAD: Right sides together, oversew one long edge of the hood around the face, leaving a gap of about 2 cm ($\frac{3}{4}$ in) between A–B. Fold the hood as broken line and join C–D. Turn to right side.

BODY: Right side inside, join between E–F to form centre front seam. Push head inside body so that right sides are together: then join lower edge of head to top edge of body, matching points C–G at back, and front seam to face mid-way between A–B. Turn body to right side.

STUFFING: Temporarily pin across point of hood, 1.5 cm ($\frac{5}{8}$ in) below tip, then stuff head fairly firmly. Stuff body more softly, lessening towards base. Matching front seam to centre back (sides as broken lines on diagram), oversew lower edge neatly.

NECK: Gather around lower edge of hood, over seam, and draw in to shape head and shoulders.

HAIR: Each bunch of curls is wool or yarn wound tightly around the tip of one finger 5–6 times: catch the loops together and stitch to the forehead, beginning at the centre and adding bunches at each side, then underneath.

EYES: Sew two black sequins to face, positioning carefully.

FEATURES: Make a tiny straight stitch in double thread for the nose. Use single thread to embroider mouths in outline or stem stitch.

TRIMMING: Stick or sew flat or gathered trimming around front edge of hood and down front of bag, following the photograph for guidance.

Moses basket

Rummage through your cuttings bag to find oddments of firm cotton or other medium-weight fabric to cover the inside and outside of the basket. Ideally, plan the baby and basket together, mixing and matching designs and colours to tone and complement each other.

MATERIALS: Thin, flexible card, 5 × 46 cm (2 × 18 in) for sides
Stiff card, 10 × 20 cm (4 × 7$\frac{1}{2}$ in) for base
Thin sheet foam—about 1 cm ($\frac{3}{8}$ in) thick—or wadding/cotton batting, to cover base
Fabric for inside—to cover sides and base
Fabric for outside—to cover sides
Felt or fabric (or heavy paper) to cover base

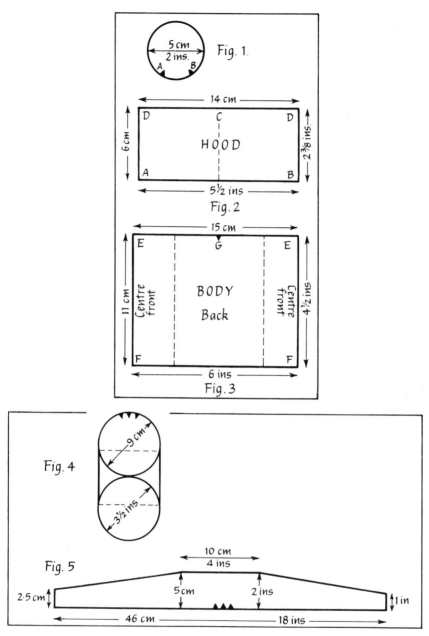

Fig. 1.

5 cm
2 ins.
A   B

14 cm

D   C   D

HOOD

6 cm

A   B

5½ ins

2⅜ ins

Fig. 2

15 cm

E   G   E

11 cm

BODY
Back

Centre front   Centre front

F   F

4½ ins

6 ins

Fig. 3

Fig. 4

9 cm

3½ ins

Fig. 5

10 cm
4 ins

5 cm   2 ins

2·5 cm   1 in

46 cm   18 ins

20

50 cm ($\frac{1}{2}$ yd) braid, lace, or similar trim for top edge
60 cm (24 in) lacing cord, narrow braid, etc for handles
Double-sided tape (optional)
All-purpose fabric adhesive

BASE: Draw shape on stiff card, following fig. 4, and cut out. Cover with foam or wadding, trimming edges level.
Cut fabric 2 cm ($\frac{3}{4}$ in) larger all round. Then cover padded surface smoothly, snipping overlapping fabric into tabs and sticking smoothly underneath.

SIDES: Cut thin card as fig. 5. Sticking lightly, cover one side with fabric to match base: trim top edge level, but allow a 1 cm ($\frac{3}{8}$ in) overlap along the lower edge—and also at *one* end. Stick lower overlap neatly to back of card.
   Cover the reverse with outer fabric, exactly as inside—overlapping lower edge, and the *other* end: stick lightly along the top edge only (use tape, if available).

ASSEMBLING: Match centre top of base to centre of lower edge of sides. Catch the two edges together round to foot of basket (avoiding outer fabric): then repeat for other side. Overlap ends and stick neatly. Then stick lower overlap to base, snipping tabs as before.
   Stick braid or alternative trimming around top edge.

HANDLES: Fix centre section of cord underneath base, 5 cm (2 in) from top, as broken line on diagram: fix ends of cord, the cut ends meeting, 5 cm (2 in) from foot (as broken line).
   Take loops up at each side to form handles, and catch to top edge.

BASE: Stick felt or fabric neatly over base, and trim level with edge.

Two more babies

NANOOK: Cosy as can be in a tartan-lined basket, and a warm gold outfit trimmed with lambswool. His dark brown hair is 5 cm (2 in) lengths of thick-knit wool or yarn, folded in half, stitched to the forehead and cut straight across, as shown.

PAPOOSE: Just omit the sides of the Moses basket—and you have a traditional Indian baby's carrying board! Join the ends of a 38 cm (15 in) length of

21

round elastic and fix across the back of the board exactly as for the handles—but so that the elastic crosses over at the front, instead of forming a loop at each side. Trim the edge with heavy rick-rack or other braid.

For the papoose, join the bag to the head so that the seam is at the centre *back*. The hair is silk lampshade fringe, and the eyes black sequins cut *almost* in half—just below the central hole. Thick-knit wool in a toning mixture of shades is twisted into a cord to edge the hood—and makes a looped fringe along the bottom of the bag (wind closely and evenly around a large knitting needle: stitch securely along lower edge of bag, then remove needle). Trim with bands of narrow braid and rick-rack.

A loop at the back of the board makes the papoose into an amusing wall decoration.

To Cuddle and Hug

Lovable rag dolls for little children

———————◆◆◆◆◆————————

The universal appeal of rag dolls ensures an eager demand: but they are *not* the quickest dolls to make. Remembering that time is money, this has to be taken into account when estimating the projected price to the customer. Also, expenses can often mount up on large dolls, if fabrics and long lengths of wide trimming have to be purchased specially.

So, adopting the maxim that 'small is profitable'; here is a rag-doll, the right size for little hands. It has all the charm of its bigger sisters, but avoids many of the disadvantages, and the boys are not forgotten either. The basic doll is small and simple and, instead of first making the figure and then dressing it, most of the garments are part of the doll itself. The only fabric you may have to buy is for the head and hands. Clothing can be snipped out of dressmaking left-overs and only short lengths of narrow trimming are needed.

The one really important rule to remember is never to hurry the stuffing. Patient, smooth, very firm stuffing—pushed well home, a little at a time—is the inside secret of every successful rag doll.

MATERIALS: Cream cotton poplin or similar fabric, for head and hands: 10.5 × 31 cm (4 × 12 in)
OR for head, hands *and* legs: 21.5 × 27 cm (8½ × 10½ in)
Fabric for body and arms: 9 × 30 cm (3½ × 11 in)
Fabric for contrast legs: 11 × 22 cm (4½ × 9 in)
OR for body, arms and matching legs: 13 × 45 cm (5 × 18 in)
Felt for shoes or slippers: 4 × 11 cm (1½ × 4½ in)
OR 22 cm (¼ yd) braid, ribbon, etc, 1 cm (⅜ in) wide, plus 2 × 10 cm (¾ × 4 in) felt for soles
Scraps of coloured and black felt for eyes
Kapok or Polyester fiberfill for stuffing

23

Black sewing thread for eyes and nose
Deep pink stranded embroidery cotton for mouth
Thick knitting wool or yarn for hair (see individual dolls)
Lolly or Popsicle stick (optional)
Stiff card for inner soles
All-purpose fabric adhesive

ADDITIONAL MATERIALS FOR INDIVIDUAL GARMENTS:

MILLIE:
Felt for pinafore: 16.5 × 11 cm (6½ × 4½ in)
15 cm (6 in) very narrow lace for collar
8 cm (3 in) narrow lace for cuffs
40 cm (16 in) narrow ribbon for hair

EDWARD:
Felt for dungarees: 14 × 18 cm (5½ × 7 in)
Scrap of felt for buttons

REBECCA:
Fabric for skirt: 12 × 30 cm (4½ × 12 in)
Fabric for pantalettes: 14 × 20 cm (5½ × 8 in)
Fabric for mob cap: 20 cm (8 in) diameter circle
Fabric for pinafore: 8 × 10 cm (3 × 4 in)
90 cm (1 yd) broderie anglaise or eyelet embroidery,
2.5 cm (1 in) deep, for cap and pinafore
50 cm (½ yd) narrow lace for pinafore and pantalettes
8 cm (3 in) narrow lace for cuffs
9 cm (3½ in) narrow braid or ribbon for collar
50 cm (½ yd) narrow ribbon for pinafore
12 cm (5 in) ribbon, 1 cm (⅜ in) wide, for cap
Narrow round elastic for cap

NOTE: *There is no seam allowance on these pattern pieces.* This is because the design can be made up in such a wide variety of fabrics. Allow about 5 mm (¼ in) all round for medium-weight, firmly woven fabrics (dress cotton, poplins, fine wool, etc). For felt, allow 2 mm (⅟₁₆ in) for seams and turnings only: cut all other edges (and also the sole) level with pattern. This also means you can draw round the edge of the pattern to mark an accurate stitching line on your fabric, if you wish.

PATTERNS: Trace *separate* patterns for the head front and back, and body front and back, following the appropriate lines. (For bare arms, trace the hand joined to the arm, and cut in one piece, in cream.)

CUTTING: Adding seam allowance as above, cut the head front and back once each, and the hand four times, in cream. Cut the remaining pieces in your chosen fabric/s: the body front and back once each, the arm four times, and the leg twice (cutting lower edge level with pattern). Cut the sole twice in felt *level with pattern*: cut twice more in card, as broken line, and stick to felt.

HEAD AND BODY: Right sides together, join the front head to the body front, and the back head to the body back, between x's.

Gather round edge of head front, beginning and ending at circles. Right sides together, pin the head pieces, matching x's and notches: draw up gathers to fit, distributing evenly between notches, then join all round, between x's.

Join sides of body below x's. Turn up a narrow hem around lower edge.

Clip neck curves, and turn to right side.

Stuff very firmly, moulding the head smoothly. Push lolly or Popsicle stick up centre of body and into head.

ARM: Right sides together, join hands to arms, then join the two pieces, leaving open between notches. Clip curves and turn to right side. Stuff, then slip-stitch opening.

LEG: Open out and stick a 1 cm (⅜ in) wide strip of felt (ribbon or braid) to the right side for shoe, top edge as broken line, lower edges level.

Right side inside, fold as pattern, and join centre front seam. Clip ankle and toe, then turn to right side. Fit sole to lower edge of foot (card inside), matching toe and centre back: oversew edges neatly together.

Stuff firmly, then stitch together across top, matching centre front seam to centre back of leg.

ASSEMBLING FIGURE: Pin the legs, side-by-side and toes forward, to the inside of the body front (check feet are level): stitch securely. Pin lower edge of body back over legs, level with front stitching line. Join across one leg, then complete stuffing body before sewing other leg.

Stitch tops of arms securely to shoulders.

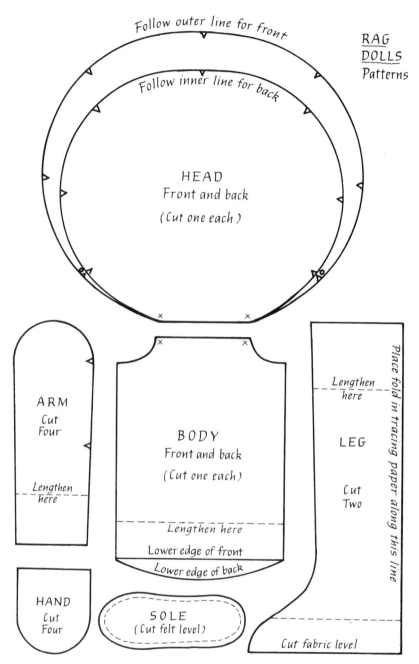

Follow outer line for front

Follow inner line for back

RAG
DOLLS
Patterns

HEAD
Front and back
(Cut one each)

ARM
Cut
Four

Lengthen
here

BODY
Front and back
(Cut one each)

Lengthen here
Lower edge of front
Lower edge of back

LEG

Cut
Two

Place fold in tracing paper along this line

Lengthen
here

HAND
Cut
Four

SOLE
(Cut felt level)

Cut fabric level

26

HAIR: See directions for individual dolls.

EYES: Cut circles of coloured felt as pattern. Pin to face, then make eight straight stitches from the centre in black thread, as indicated. Cut (or punch) pupils in black felt: position at centre of eye—then make eight more stitches, exactly over the previous ones, but this time including the pupil.

NOSE: Make a tiny straight stitch in double black thread.

MOUTH: Mark curve lightly in pencil: embroider in outline or stem stitch, using two strands of cotton.

Millie

A tiny felt pinafore dress and an impish grin make Millie a thoroughly modern M/s!

FIGURE: Make the body, arms and legs in flowered dress cotton. Gather lace around neck for collar. Trim wrists with lace to match pinafore.

PINAFORE: Cut twice in felt. Join side seams and turn to right side. Fit on doll, overlap felt on shoulders, and stitch.

HAIR: Use *very* thick (double-double) wool or yarn. Keep adding sets of four strands, as directed below, stitching them closely together so that the head is completely covered.

Mark forehead 3.5 cm (1½ in) below centre of top seam. Cut four 40 cm (15 in) strands of wool and stitch centre *flat* across the mark: then take each half smoothly down across face and stitch over side seam (fig. 1).

Stitch another four strands immediately above the first ones: take each side down across face as before, but catch strands tightly together over the seam, above the previous ones.

Repeat in this way until top seam is covered. Continue down back of head, but take the next two or three sets of strands across each side of the head—and then round to the front, over the first ones, and catch just in front of them. Divide hanging strands equally into three and plait neatly: bind ends tightly, and trim level.

Cut an 8 cm (3 in) deep piece of card, and wind wool smoothly around it 6–8 times. Catch loops tightly together at each edge, then slide off card.

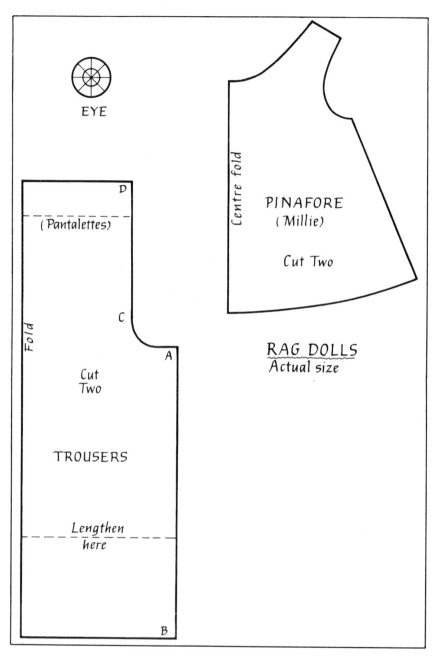

EYE

D

(Pantalettes)

Centre fold

PINAFORE
(Millie)

Cut Two

Fold

C

A

Cut
Two

RAG DOLLS
Actual size

TROUSERS

Lengthen
here

B

28

Stretch across to cover back of head: stitch each side immediately behind plait—then spread strands smoothly and stitch down centre.

Tie plaits with 20 cm (8 in) lengths of ribbon.

Edward

Edward is every inch the mischievous tomboy, but he's the same doll with dungarees and a different hairstyle.

FIGURE: Make the body, arms and legs in plaid fabric.

DUNGAREES: Cut trouser leg twice in felt. Cut straps 1 cm ($\frac{3}{8}$ in) wide × 10 cm (4 in) long.

Right side inside, fold each leg in half and join side seam between A–B. Right sides together, join the two pieces between A–D for centre front seam. But join only between A–C for back. Turn to right side, fit on doll and slip-stitch remainder of centre back seam.

Fit straps over shoulders as shown, crossing at back. Tuck ends inside trousers at back, and sew. Round ends at front and catch into place with a tiny 'button' punched from felt.

HAIR: The little boy in the picture has a tousled style made from 'double-knitting' wool. You may need to adjust the number of times you wind it around the card, depending on the weight of your own wool or yarn: experiment, using the illustration for guidance.

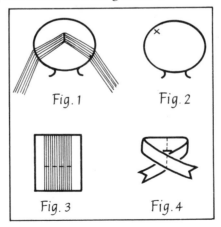

Fig. 1   Fig. 2

Fig. 3   Fig. 4

29

Wind wool or yarn 10 times around an 8 cm (3 in) deep card: tie the loops at one edge—then cut them along the other edge. Stitch the tied section to the front of the head, against the seam, at x on fig. 2.

Stitch a similar set of loops to the back of the head, close behind the first ones. Then repeat at other side of head.

Wind wool or yarn very evenly 25 times around a 15 cm (6 in) deep card. Run a thread through the strands on one side, 6 cm (2¼ in) above lower edge (fig. 3). Cut loops at each end, remove card and stitch across again, to hold strands together. Place this piece over top of head, covering forehead as shown: stitch securely over seam.

Smooth strands all round head, sticking lightly underneath. Trim ends neatly to shape.

Rebecca

She has all the characteristic charm of the traditional rag doll, so you'll have to allow a little more time for Victorian frills and flounces. As an attractive and time-saving alternative, you could omit the pantalettes, and make her stockinged legs in a contrasting fabric with narrow horizontal stripes.

FIGURE: Make the body, arms and legs in plain fabric.

PANTALETTES: Cut the leg twice in fabric with the waist 1 cm (⅜ in) lower as shown by dotted line on pattern. Make up as Edward's dungarees, but clip curve before turning to right side. Turn under top edge and turn up lower edges, then fit on doll and slip-stitch remainder of seam. Trim lower edges with lace.

SKIRT: Right side inside, join the short side edges of the skirt to form centre back seam. Turn to right side. Turn under top edge and gather. Mark centre front and sides, then fit on doll and draw up around body, close under arms: distribute gathers evenly, then stitch securely into place. Turn up hem.

COLLAR AND CUFFS: Trim neck and wrists with braid and lace, as shown.

PINAFORE: Turn under side and lower edges and trim with lace. Gather top edge and draw up to measure 5 cm (2 in). Slip-stitch lower edge of ribbon over gathers, matching centres, so ribbon extends equally each side.

Cut straps 8 cm (3 in) long. Turn under raw edge and gather, then draw up over each shoulder, stitching ends to waist at front and back, as illustrated. Tie pinafore around waist.

HAIR: This style again uses a very thick 'double-double' knitting wool: adjust as before for a lighter-weight wool or yarn.

Wind wool or yarn very evenly 10 times around a 15 cm (6 in) deep card. Run a thread through the strands on one side, 6 cm ($2\frac{1}{4}$ in) above lower edge (see fig. 3 on page 29). Tie loops loosely at top edge, and cut across bottom.

Place over top of head, cut ends overlapping forehead. Catch loops securely, spreading across nape of neck and removing tie as you do so. Smooth up over back of head, and stitch across top, covering centre 5 cm (2 in) of seam.

Wind wool or yarn 6 times around the same card. Catch loops tightly at each edge, then remove card and catch tightly around centre. Stitch centre over seam at one side of head, close against previous section: then take ends down to cover front and back, and stitch neatly.

Repeat for other side. Trim fringe.

MOB CAP: *Wrong sides together*, stitch trimming around edge of fabric, *outer* edge of trimming towards centre of circle. Fold over along stitching line, raw edges inside, and stitch again to form a narrow channel. Thread elastic through and draw up to fit head.

Fold ribbon as fig. 4. Gather as broken line, then draw up tightly and bind with thread. Stitch to cap.

Ready for Play

Tough companions for energetic youngsters

———◆◆◆◆►———

These cheerful characters are designed with boys in mind. They're made of felt, with bright, bold colours and firm strength to stand up to plenty of hard play.

The basic doll is the same as that in the last chapter, but a little longer in body and limb. Nevertheless, amounts of materials still remain comparatively small. Felt is a worthwhile investment when time is money: no hems or seams to clip, no fraying, and patterns can be placed in any direction. (Keep a 'bits box' for scraps—any cutting over 1 cm square.) Finally, it's the ideal medium for anyone with little or no experience of toy-making. The firm, even texture makes it a pleasure to work with: seams are oversewn, and it moulds easily to a softly rounded shape when firmly stuffed.

Just a word of warning. It is tempting to use shiny brass buttons, wooden beads and similar trimmings to make this type of character doll even more fun. But these can be dangerous in the hands of very small children, who tend to suck, chew and swallow the most unappetising things.

PATTERNS: Follow directions for the rag doll (p. 26), using the same pattern pieces BUT *add 2.5 cm (1 in) to the length of the two body pieces, the arm, the leg and the trousers* (do this at points indicated by heavy broken lines).

SEAM ALLOWANCE: Add 2 mm ($\frac{1}{16}$ in) to felt for joins, but cut all other edges level (including sole). Oversew edges—and ignore instructions for turning up hems, clipping turnings, etc.

Captain Courage on Parade

Lots of silky gold braid is essential to make him the pride of the regiment. Ideally, look for a narrow lampshade braid which can be cut in half down the centre: use it both full-width and half-width, as illustrated.

Rebecca and Dingleweed, the gnome

Captain Courage and Blueberry, the mischievous elf

MATERIALS: Flesh felt for head and hands: 14 × 19 cm (5½ × 7½ in)
Blue felt for jacket: 18 × 23 cm (7 × 9 in)
Red felt for jacket: 10 cm (4 in) square
Black felt for legs, cap and eyes: 25 cm (10 in) square
Light grey felt for trousers: 15 × 20 cm (6 × 8 in)
Mid-brown felt for hair: 3 × 14 cm (1¼ × 5½ in)
Scrap of dark brown felt for moustache
Gold felt for cap: 5 cm (2 in) diameter circle
Small lace motif or alternative for cap 'badge'
80 cm (⅞ yd) silky gold braid about 1 cm (⅜ in) *full-width* (to
be cut in half, as above, for very narrow decoration)
OR 40 cm (15 in) braid, about 1 cm (⅜ in) wide, and 90 cm
(1 yd) very narrow braid
30 cm (12 in) narrow black braid for trousers
Kapok or Polyester fiberfill for stuffing
Lolly or Popsicle stick (optional)
Flexible card for cap (cereal carton, etc)
Scrap of stiff card for soles
All-purpose fabric adhesive

CUTTING: Cut the head front and back once each, and the hand four times, in flesh. Cut the body front and back once each, the arm four times, and the jacket flap once, in blue. Cut the facing panel once and the epaulette and cuff twice each, in red. Cut the leg and sole twice each in black: cut the sole twice more in stiff card, as broken line, and stick to felt.

HEAD AND BODY: As rag doll (p. 25)—but appliqué (or stick) facing panel to centre front, *after* joining body to head. Continue as directed.

ARM: As rag doll (p. 25).

LEG: Fold as pattern and join centre front seam. Turn to right side. Fit sole to lower edge of foot (card inside), matching toe and centre back: oversew edges neatly together.

Stuff firmly, then stitch together across top, matching centre front seam to centre back of leg.

ASSEMBLING FIGURE: As rag doll (p. 25).

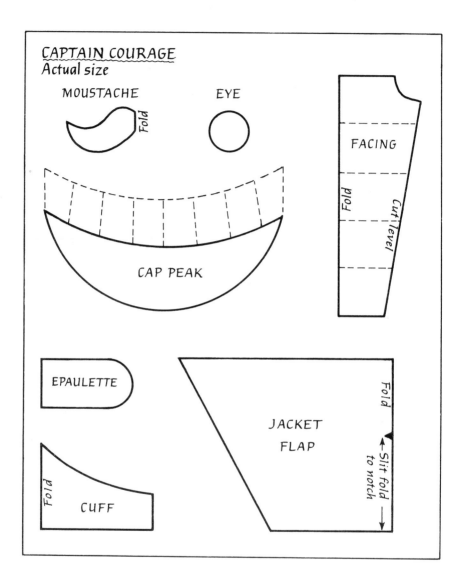

CAPTAIN COURAGE
Actual size

MOUSTACHE

EYE

Fold

CAP PEAK

FACING

Fold

Cut level

EPAULETTE

JACKET FLAP

Fold

Slit fold to notch

CUFF

Fold

TROUSERS: Follow directions for Edward's dungarees (p. 29)—omitting the straps, but adding a band of black braid down each side. Stitch top edge to figure at waist level.

JACKET FLAP: Stitch top edge to body, over trousers: front corners meeting corners of facing panel.

FACING PANEL: Stick horizontal bands of very narrow braid across, as indicated: then along sides and lower edge.

EPAULETTES: Stick very narrow braid around outer edge, then stitch short straight edge close to neck.

COLLAR: Stick full-width braid around neck.

CUFFS: Stick around wrists: trim top edge with very narrow braid.

HAIR: Appliqué (or stick) around head, drawing lower edge round towards front, as illustrated.

CAP: Stick a strip of card, 5 × 23 cm (2 × 9 in), to black felt: cut felt level, but leave a 1 cm (½ in) overlap at one short end. Fit snugly around head, mark overlap at centre back, and then stick join securely.

Cut the peak in card and stick to felt: cut felt level all round. Stick other side of card to felt: cut outer curve level again—but cut inner curve as broken line, snipping this surplus into tabs, as indicated.

Fit peak level with lower edge at centre front of cap, sticking tabs smoothly up inside. (Blacken cut edge of card with a marker or felt pen if it is unsightly.)

Place cap upside-down on card, and draw around outside. Cut out card oval and stick to felt: cut felt fractionally larger than card. Pin to top of cap, then oversew edges neatly together all round.

In gold felt, cut around a 4 cm (1½ in) diameter circle with pinking shears: stick to centre front of cap. Stick full-width braid around lower edge, then decorate circle with narrow braid around central motif.

Stick narrow braid around face for chin-strap, ends level with top edge of hair at each side. Then stick hat securely to head.

FEATURES: Stick eyes and moustache into position, following the picture.

Cowboy Larry

All the way from the Wild West: that broad grin obviously means he's just carried off every prize at the rodeo!

MATERIALS: Flesh felt for head and hands: 14 × 19 cm (5$\frac{1}{2}$ × 7$\frac{1}{2}$ in)
Yellow felt for shirt: 22 × 16 cm (8$\frac{1}{2}$ × 6$\frac{1}{2}$ in)
Light brown felt for legs: 15 × 20 cm (6 × 8 in)
Mid-brown felt for pants: 15 × 20 cm (6 × 8 in)
Dark brown felt for hat and soles: 25 cm (10 in) square
Orange felt for waistcoat/vest: 13 × 8 cm (5 × 3 in)
Green felt for neckerchief: see directions
Scrap of gold felt for buttons
Scrap of black felt for eyes
18 cm (7 in) stiff petersham ribbon, 1.5 cm ($\frac{5}{8}$ in) wide, for belt
10 cm (4 in) very narrow braid, for buckle
25 cm (9 in) narrow rick-rack braid to trim waistcoat/vest
Thick wool or yarn for hair
Stranded embroidery cotton for mouth
Black sewing thread for nose
Kapok or Polyester fiberfill for stuffing
Lolly or Popsicle stick (optional)
Scrap of stiff card for soles
All-purpose fabric adhesive

CUTTING: Cut the head front and back once each, and the hand four times, in flesh. Cut the body back and front once each, and the arm four times, in yellow. Cut the leg twice in light brown, and the sole twice in dark brown: cut the sole twice more in stiff card, as broken line, and stick to felt.

HEAD AND BODY: As rag doll (p. 25).

ARM: As rag doll (p. 25).

LEG: As soldier doll (p. 33).

ASSEMBLING FIGURE: As rag doll (p. 25).

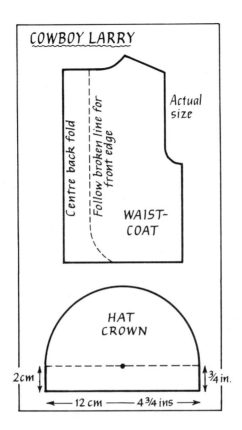

COWBOY LARRY

Actual size

Centre back fold

Follow broken line for front edge

WAIST-COAT

HAT CROWN

2cm | ¾ in.

←— 12 cm —— 4 ¾ ins —→

PANTS: Lengthen trouser-leg pattern (p. 28) as directed at beginning of this chapter: *but also* cut the top edge 1 cm (⅜ in) lower.

Follow directions for Edward's dungarees (p. 29)—omitting the straps. Stitch top edge to figure at hip level.

BELT: Stick petersham ribbon around top of pants. Then stick narrow braid in buckle shape, as illustrated.

SHIRT: Punch tiny circles of gold felt for buttons, and stick down centre front. Stick 1.5 cm (½ in) wide strips of felt around wrists, for cuffs.

WAISTCOAT/VEST: Cut the back once and front twice. Join side and shoulder seams and turn to right side. Stick rick-rack around edge.

37

NECKERCHIEF: Fold a 6 cm (2½ in) square of paper in half diagonally for pattern to cut felt. Catch corners of triangle together at back of neck.

HAIR: Doll illustrated is as Edward in previous chapter, but uses thicker (double-double) knitting wool. Adjust directions on page 29, according to weight of wool or yarn.

HAT: Cut a 15 cm (6 in) diameter circle for the brim, with a 7 cm (2¾ in) diameter hole in the centre. For crown pattern, draw a 12 cm (4¾ in) diameter semi-circle, adding 2 cm (¾ in) at the base: cut twice in felt.

   Join the two crown pieces, leaving straight lower edge open. Turn to right side. Pin inner edge of brim evenly round lower edge of crown, top of brim against right side of crown: oversew neatly.

   Pinch seam together inside top of crown, and stitch pleat to hold. Catch brim up at each side. Fit hat on doll and catch into position.

FEATURES: Stick circles of black felt (as soldier) to face for eyes. Embroider mouth in outline or stem stitch, using three strands of embroidery cotton. Make a single straight stitch in double thread for nose.

Blueberry, the mischievous elf

The ideal present for a child with parent problems. Any mysterious happenings which demand explanation can be blamed on Blueberry: up to his tricks again!

   He's also a wonderful opportunity for artistic colour combinations: the bright yellowy-greens of spring—the russets and golds of falling leaves—the pinks, plums and purple of ripening fruit—or the mellow browns of acorns, chestnuts and dark tree-trunks.

   His boots are optional. They continue the petal theme of the costume but if you want to save time, leave his feet uncovered or make tiny slippers from straight strips of felt or ribbon as directed on p. 25 (see Leg).

MATERIALS: Flesh felt for head and hands: 14 × 19 cm (5½ × 7½ in)
Light turquoise blue felt for body, hat and boots: 25 cm (10 in) square
Deep turquoise blue felt for arms, hat, collar, etc: 20 cm (8 in) square
Blue-green felt for legs and hat: 18 × 20 cm (7 × 8 in)
Scrap of brown felt for soles

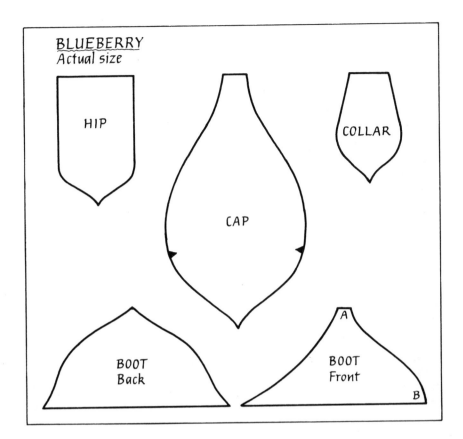

BLUEBERRY
Actual size

HIP

CAP

COLLAR

BOOT
Back

BOOT
Front

A

B

Scrap of black felt for eyes
15 cm (6 in) embroidered flower trimming for waist
Thick knitting wool or yarn for hair
Stranded embroidery cotton for mouth
Black sewing thread for nose
Kapok or Polyester fiberfill for stuffing
Lolly or Popsicle stick (optional)
Scrap of stiff card for soles
All-purpose fabric adhesive

CUTTING: Cut the head front and back once each, and the hand four times, in flesh. Cut the body front and back once each, in light blue. Cut the arm four

39

times in deep blue. Cut the leg twice in green, and the sole twice in brown: cut the sole twice more in stiff card, as broken line, and stick to felt.

HEAD AND BODY: As rag doll (p. 25).

ARM: As rag doll (p. 25).

LEG: As soldier doll (p. 33).

ASSEMBLING FIGURE: As rag doll (p. 25).

HIP DECORATION: Cut hip petal six times each in light and deep blue. Pin the light petals, side-by-side, around body, 2.5 cm (1 in) above lower edge (at front)—positioned so that petals meet at centre front and back, and one covers each side seam: stitch top edge to body. Now pin the darker petals over the light ones, positioning as illustrated, with the top edge just above the previous ones: stitch to body as before. Stick trimming around waist.

COLLAR: Cut collar petal six times in deep blue. Pin around neck as illustrated, then stitch top edge: stick upper half of each petal lightly to body.

BOOT: Cut the front twice and back once, in light blue (turnings *are* allowed).
Right sides together, join front pieces between A–B. Turn to right side and pin over foot, seams matching: oversew straight edge neatly to edge of sole. Fit back section around back of foot: oversew lower edge to sole—overlapping front of boot at each side.

HAIR: Doll illustrated is as Edward in previous chapter (p. 29). Adjust directions, if necessary, according to weight of wool or yarn you are using.

CAP: Cut cap petal three times each in light and deep blue (turnings *are* allowed). Oversew neatly together, side-by-side in alternate shades, between top corner and notch. Join first petal to last, and turn to right side.
For the stalk, cut a strip of green felt 3 × 5 cm (1¼ × 2 in): roll up, and oversew join. Push up through centre of cap, leaving 5 mm (¼ in) inside: stitch firmly into place.
Stick cap securely to head.

FEATURES: As cowboy (p. 38).

Jamie—the winter sports enthusiast

Jamie's warm as toast in his cosy outfit, with a long woolly muffler—and matching hat pulled down over his ears. Save money by knitting up oddments of wool or yarn to make his accessories: or buy a suitable woven braid, instead. 'Mixing and matching' is the secret of Jamie's eye-catching appeal: smooth felt in three shades of one colour—teamed with the uneven texture and sharply contrasting colour-scheme of the knitted accessories.

MATERIALS: Flesh felt for head: 10 × 20 cm (4 × 8 in)
Light orange felt for hat and mittens: 20 cm (8 in) square
Mid-orange felt for top: 23 × 25 cm (9 × 10 in)
Deep orange felt for trousers: 13 × 20 cm (5 × 8 in)
Dark brown felt for legs (boots): 20 cm (8 in) square
Scrap of black felt for eyes
Thick knitting wool or yarn for hair
Novelty knitting wool or yarn in contrasting colour/s for scarf, hat and cuffs
10 cm (4 in) fringe, 2.5 cm (1 in) deep, to trim scarf
Black sewing thread for nose
Kapok or Polyester fiberfill for stuffing
Lolly or Popsicle stick (optional)
Scrap of stiff card for soles
All-purpose fabric adhesive

CUTTING: Cut the head back and front once each, in flesh. Cut the body back and front, and the top (fig. 1), once each, and the arm four times, in mid-orange. Cut the hand four times in light orange, and also two pieces 8 × 15 cm (3 × 6 in), for the hat. Cut the leg and sole twice each in brown: cut the sole twice more in stiff card, as broken line, and stick to felt.

HEAD AND BODY: As rag doll (p. 25).

ARM: As rag doll (p. 25).

LEG: As soldier doll (p. 33).

ASSEMBLING FIGURE: As rag doll (p. 25).

41

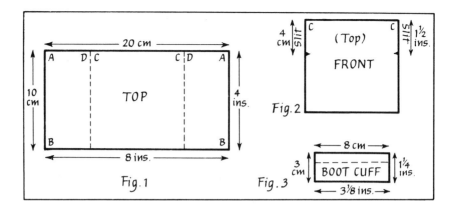

TROUSERS: *Do not lengthen* trouser-leg pattern (p. 28) as instructed at beginning of this chapter: cut original version twice in deep orange.

Follow directions for Edward's dungarees (p. 29), omitting straps. Stitch top edge to figure at waist level. Then gather each lower edge and draw up tightly around legs, pushing up slightly, as illustrated.

BOOTS: Cut cuff (fig. 3) twice in dark brown. Fold under 1 cm ($\frac{1}{2}$ in) at top (broken line) and stick around leg, over trouser gathers: oversew join at centre back (trim off excess, if necessary).

TOP: Join side edges (A–B) to form centre back seam, and turn to right side. Slit fold 4 cm ($1\frac{1}{2}$ in) at each side (fig. 2) for armholes. Fit on doll, lapping top corners C over back corners D: slip-stitch edge of armhole over seam at top of arm. Then gather top edge and draw up to fit.

HAIR: Doll illustrated is as Edward in previous chapter (p. 29), but uses thicker (double-double) knitting wool. Adjust directions according to weight of wool or yarn.

HAT: Join short edges of felt to form side seams. Gather top edge and draw up as tightly as possible, catching gathered edge together before turning to right side.

According to thickness of wool or yarn, needle size and tension, cast on appropriate number of stitches to knit a strip 4 cm ($1\frac{1}{2}$ in) wide. Continue knitting until strip is 25 cm (10 in) long: cast off.

Join short ends of knitted strip to form band, and stitch one long edge just inside lower edge of hat: then turn up as illustrated. Make a pompon in the usual way, using 6 cm (2¼ in) circles of card, with a 2 cm (¾ in) hole in the centre. Trim neatly and stitch on top.

Fit hat on doll and catch securely to head.

SCARF: Knit a strip the same width as above, but 35 cm (14 in) long. Trim ends with fringe. Knot around neck as illustrated, catching to felt to hold in place.

CUFFS: Knit two strips *half* the width of hat-band and scarf, and about 7–8 cm (3 in) long. Join short ends of each, and stick or stitch around wrists.

EYES AND NOSE: As cowboy (p. 38).

And now ... Dolls for Everyone!

A simple basis for endless adaptation

The preceding dolls have all been planned specifically for children, but the appeal of dolls extends to all ages and the scope is unlimited. Hazards that must be avoided in dolls for young children no longer apply: tiny beads, buttons and delicate trimmings can all be used to fashion amusing characters with the persuasive charm to capture a ready market.

For the second half of the book, I have designed a small basic figure which is extremely quick and easy to make, and can achieve any amount of animation. The clothes themselves play a major part in determining the actual shape: the rest lies in clever characterisation. Obviously my own examples are only the tip of a creative iceberg. Your own imagination, picture books, television and the people you meet in the street will supply endless characters to be re-created as the kind of little figure that will sit happily on a bookshelf, desk or dressing table, beside a bed, on the kitchen wall, at school, in a den, work-room, greenhouse—or in the car. They have a novelty value which gives as much satisfaction and pleasure to the giver as the recipient, which can make them the ideal present for a surprising number of 'people who have every-thing'.

Full directions are given for a varied selection of characters, designed to attract a wide range of tastes and interests. Alternatively, use the basic figure and alter the patterns and other individual directions to produce the kind of dolls which you think will be the greatest draw for your own particular market. The cover photograph shows three examples of how this can be done: Merlin, the wizard, the splendid genie and the egg-head professor are the same doll with clothes adapted from the patterns on the following pages.

The basic figure

Before beginning the figure, it is important to check the individual directions for the character you are planning to make. The 'Basic doll' paragraph for each character explains any special adjustments that need to be made: which version of the body pattern to use, and how to cut the foot.

In the following instructions, 1 cm (⅜ in) thick sheet foam is specified for the body and limbs. Alternatively, substitute ordinary wadding or cotton batting.

MATERIALS: Flesh felt for head, etc: see directions for individual doll
Felt for feet, shoes, boots, etc: see directions for individual doll
Felt for soles: see directions for individual doll
Foam sheet, 1 cm (⅜ in) thick (or alternative) for body and limbs: 11 × 25 cm (5 × 10 in)—*plus* 4 × 7 cm (1½ × 2¾ in) for stouter doll

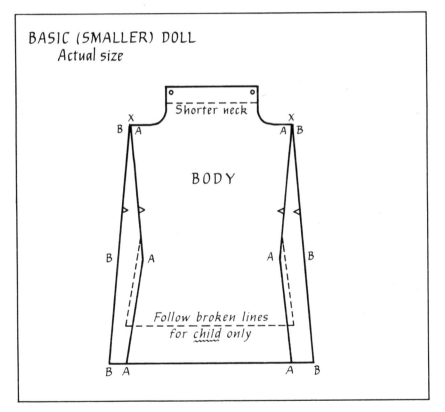

BASIC (SMALLER) DOLL
Actual size

Shorter neck

BODY

Follow broken lines
for child only

Kapok or Polyester fiberfill to stuff head
3½ pipe cleaners: 16.5 cm (6½ in) long
Knitting wool or yarn for hair: see individual doll
Stiff card for inner soles
All-purpose fabric adhesive

FOAM: Prepare pieces as diagrams: cut the body, arms and neck once each, and the leg twice. Cut the inner body only if making the stouter figure (B).

LEGS: For each, wrap foam around a pipe cleaner: base of leg level with one end of cleaner, the other end protruding at the top. Oversew long edges of

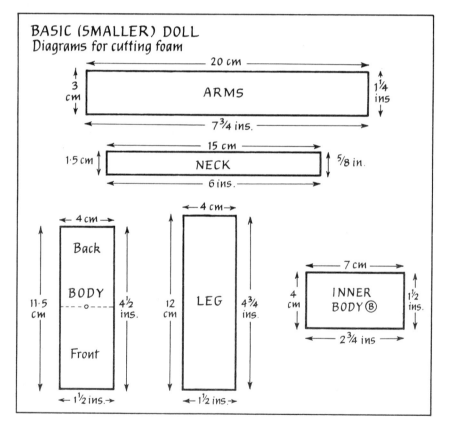

BASIC (SMALLER) DOLL
Diagrams for cutting foam

ARMS — 20 cm — 7¾ ins. — 3 cm / 1¼ ins

NECK — 15 cm — 6 ins. — 1·5 cm / ⅝ in.

BODY (Back / Front) — 4 cm — 11·5 cm — 4½ ins. — 1½ ins.

LEG — 4 cm — 12 cm — 4¾ ins. — 1½ ins.

INNER BODY Ⓑ — 7 cm — 4 cm / 1½ ins — 2¾ ins

foam for centre back join. Turn back 1.5 cm ($\frac{5}{8}$ in) at top of cleaner to form a hook (fig. 1, p. 49).

NECK (I): Bend an 8 cm ($3\frac{1}{4}$ in) length of pipe cleaner in half. Hook the legs through the loop—then bend the hooks round to secure (fig. 2).

ARMS: Snip off corners of foam as indicated. Place pipe cleaner in centre (fig. 3): fold foam around it and oversew edges (fig. 4).

Now place centre of arms over point where legs join neck: bind tightly with thread (fig. 5).

INNER BODY—FIGURE B ONLY: Wrap foam around body, close under arms, and join short edges at back (fig. 6).

BODY: Make a hole in the centre, as on pattern, and push ends of neck cleaner through. Fold (as broken line) over arms, and catch lower corners of front and back together at each side (fig. 7).

NECK (II): Wind foam tightly around protruding cleaners, and secure end (fig. 7).

FELT: Trace patterns. For a slender figure, follow lines A for the sides of the body: for a stout figure, follow lines B (these are referred to as Body A and Body B in the directions for the individual characters): note also alternative neck lengths. (The lower broken lines are for a child, see p. 73.)

FLESH FELT: Cut the head front and back once each, and the body twice: add markings. Cut the hand twice, using the paper pattern—then cut twice more, this time using the *felt* shapes as patterns: leave pinned together.

BODY: Right sides together, join the front head to the neck of one body piece, between circles. Right sides together, join the second body piece to the first, oversewing neck and shoulders between o–x. Turn body to right side.

HEAD: Gather all round outer edge of front, as indicated. Right sides together, pin back and front together, matching notches and circles. Draw up

47

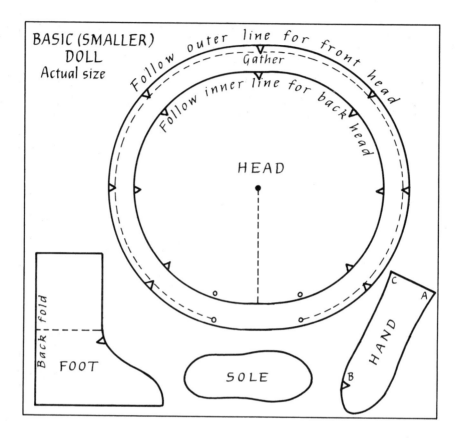

BASIC (SMALLER) DOLL
Actual size

Follow outer line for front head

Gather

Follow inner line for back head

HEAD

FOOT

Back fold

SOLE

HAND

C

A

B

gathers to fit, distributing evenly between pins: then oversew securely together all round.

Slit back of head from base to centre dot, as broken line, and turn to right side: then put slit edges together again and slip-stitch neatly. Finally, slip-stitch back of head to body across neck.

Stuff head firmly.

ASSEMBLING FIGURE: With pointed scissors or a knitting needle, drive a hole up towards the centre of the head stuffing: then push neck pipe cleaners firmly in, until neck foam is in position.

Join side edges of body below arms, between notch and bottom corner (fig. 8, p. 50).

48

Nanny Toogood and the Twins, with Bridesmaid Posy

Alexander and Eliza-Kate

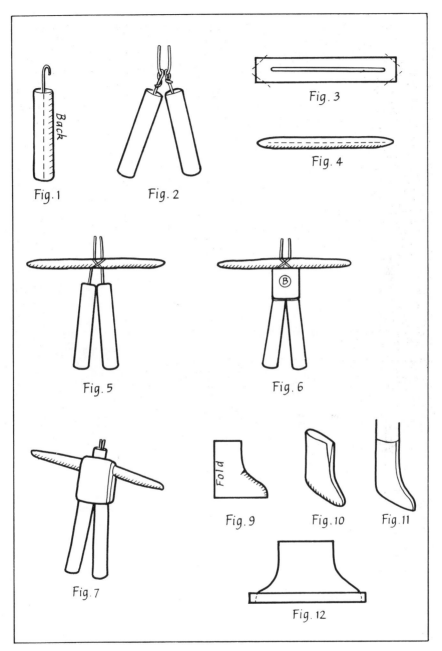

Fig. 1

Back

Fig. 2

Fig. 3

Fig. 4

Fig. 5

Fig. 6

Ⓑ

Fig. 7

Fig. 9

Fold

Fig. 10

Fig. 11

Fig. 12

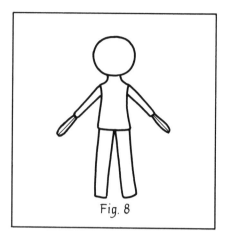

Fig. 8

HANDS: Oversew together (with tiny stitches) between A–B—then un-pin and place end of arm inside (palm down): pinch foam tightly between felt, and finish oversewing to C. Catch top of felt securely to foam (fig. 8).

FEET: If the character is wearing *boots*, cut the foot in felt of the desired colour, and the sole in the same felt, or an appropriate contrast (brown, black, grey). Cut the sole again, slightly smaller, in card: stick to felt sole.

Wrong side inside, fold the foot in half and oversew neatly between notch and toe (fig. 9). Now, matching centre back and tip of toe, fit lower edge of foot around sole, card inside, and oversew neatly together (fig. 10).

Stuff front half of foot with a scrap of foam or other filling, pushing it well down into the toe. Then fit the bottom of the leg neatly inside, making sure the base touches the sole: oversew front edges together above notch (fig. 11), and catch top of felt to foam.

Shoes, or dainty pumps, can be made as for the rag dolls on page 23. Use a strip of ribbon, braid, felt, etc—about 5 mm (¼ in) wide. Cut the foot in either flesh felt, or an appropriate colour for socks or stockings: then stick the shoe strip along the base of the foot, level with the lower edge, and overlapping each end (fig. 12). Trim surplus level with felt, then make up as above. Alternatively, stick narrow braid, ribbon etc, around the foot when it is made up (see Posy, p. 69).

50

Faces and features

The dolls for children all clearly demonstrate my own personal view that faces should be as simple and straightforward as possible. Just a few stitches are usually enough to indicate the necessary features. This is *not* merely an economy of time and effort. For example, in the case of the more sophisticated dolls which follow, just the eyes alone may prove far more alluring than a laboriously detailed face—which can also prove a time-consuming test of one's artistic abilities. Immediately you add a mouth you form an expression conveying a definite mood or personality. But with just a pair of large, intriguing eyes, the face has an enigmatic quality—an air of mystery, which can often be much more compelling than a set expression.

The eyes alone can say it all. They must be large and lustrous: so important that they command attention without the aid of other features. This can sometimes be done simply by embroidery, or with circles of plain black felt (as in the previous chapter): in other cases, domed black sequins are very effective. Another method combines black felt and small, domed sequins: these may be any suitable 'eye' colour, but I prefer a subtle, almost black mixture of very dark blue-green-purple.

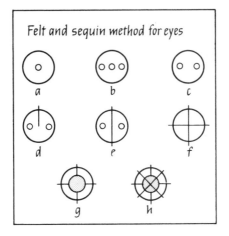

For a doll of this size, cut an 8 mm ($\frac{5}{16}$ in) diameter circle of black felt for each eye. Pin to the face to determine position (a). When satisfied, add pins at each side (b): then remove centre one (c). Using ordinary black sewing thread, drive needle into side of face (under hair) and come up in centre of eye.

Make a long straight stitch up—ending just beyond edge of circle (d). Return to centre and make a similar stitch down (e). Remove the pins, then make stitches to left and right (f). Come up through centre of felt again—and also through centre of sequin (g): make four more stitches, as before, but diagonally, between the first ones, and taking in the sequin (h). Finish off at side, and cut threads close.

Selecting fabrics

When dressing, use felts and non-woven interlinings, or choose fabrics which do not fray easily, in order to avoid having to make hems. Cut fabrics straight along the line of the weave, when possible, and draw threads to give a firm edge. If a hem *is* necessary, allow extra for turnings, when cutting out.

Trousers—Pantalettes—Pantaloons—Basic pattern

TROUSERS: Cut the pattern piece twice, shortening if necessary.

Right side inside, fold each leg in half and oversew side seam A–B. Right sides together, join the two pieces between A–D for centre front seam: but join only between A–C for back. Turn to right side, fit on doll, and slip-stitch remainder of centre back seam. Catch top edge around waist, easing gently, if necessary.

PANTALETTES/PANTALOONS: Follow above directions, adjusting length of leg, as indicated.

Leave lower edge plain, or trim with lace. Then either gather and draw up tightly around each ankle, or allow to hang freely, as appropriate for the doll concerned.

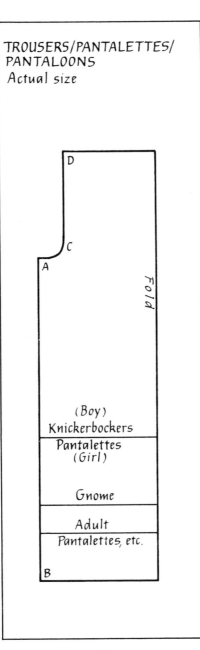

TROUSERS/PANTALETTES/
PANTALOONS
Actual size

D

C

A

Fold

(Boy)
Knickerbockers

Pantalettes
(Girl)

Gnome

Adult

Pantalettes, etc.

B

A Touch of Magic

Everybody needs a mascot

———◆◆◆◆———

Fame, fortune or romance: everyone needs a mascot! Three very different characters demonstrate the versatility of the basic doll in the previous chapter.

Gipsy Crystal Rose

What does the future hold ... what mysterious message can the gipsy see in her crystal ball?

MATERIALS: Dusky flesh felt for head, body and hands: 15 cm (6 in) square
Black felt for boots: 9 × 8 cm (3½ × 3 in)
Brown (or black) felt for soles: 4 cm (1½ in) square
Felt for bodice: 9 × 15 cm (3½ × 6 in)
Fabric for petticoat: 12 × 25 cm (4¾ × 10 in)
Fabric for skirt: 11 × 28 cm (4¼ × 11 in)
Fabric for apron: 9 cm (3½ in) square
Fabric for shawl: 11 cm (4¼ in) square
Fabric for headscarf: see fig. 1
Gold sequins or beads, etc, to trim bodice
2 small gold curtain rings (or thread circles of tiny beads) for ear-rings
2 black sequins for eyes, about 7 mm (¼ in) diameter (optional)
Medium-weight black knitting wool or yarn for hair
Large marble or small plastic or table-tennis ball

BASIC DOLL: Make as directed (p. 44), with Body A: cut the whole foot in black, for boots.

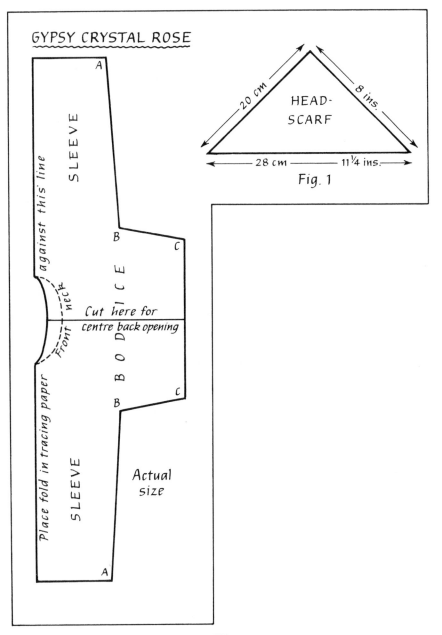

GYPSY CRYSTAL ROSE

A

SLEEVE

Place fold in tracing paper against this line

Front neck

B

C

B O D I C E

Cut here for
centre back opening

C

B

SLEEVE

Actual
size

A

HEAD-
SCARF

20 cm

8 ins.

28 cm

11¼ ins.

Fig. 1

55

PETTICOAT: Join short side edges to form centre back seam, and turn to right side. Gather top edge: mark centre front and sides, then fit on doll and draw up around waist, distributing gathers evenly. Catch into place.

SKIRT: As petticoat.

APRON: Gather top edge: draw up over waist gathers of skirt front, and catch into place.

BODICE: Cut in felt. Join sleeve and side seams A–B–C, and turn to right side. Stitch sequins or other decoration around neck and wrist edges.

Fit on doll and pin into position: slip-stitch centre back opening, then catch lower edge around waist over skirt and apron.

SHAWL: Draw threads to form fringed edge. Fold in half diagonally and drape around shoulders: catch corners together at centre front.

HAIR: 'Double-knitting' wool was used for the doll illustrated—but choose whatever wool or yarn you consider suitable, adjusting the number of times you wind it around the card accordingly. Use a single (or divided) strand to tie.

Wind wool or yarn six times around a 13 cm (5 in) deep card: tie the loops tightly at each edge with a strand of matching wool, then remove card and tie the skein loosely around the centre. Stick tied centre to front of head, against the seam: take the ends smoothly down at each side, and stitch to head.

Make another skein as above. Stick centre in front of, and against, first piece: then take ends down at each side, across ends of previous piece, and stitch over seam.

Make a third skein but this time *tie the sides loosely*, and the *centre tightly*. Catch centre to top of head, immediately behind the first piece. Then take the ends down to cover each side of back of head, and catch neatly at neck level.

Finally wind wool or yarn six times around an 11.5 cm (4½ in) card, and tie as last skein. Catch centre to crown, just behind last piece, and take ends down to fill in centre back of head, catching neatly across neck.

EAR-RINGS: Stitch curtain rings or circles of tiny gilt beads at sides of face, as illustrated.

HEADSCARF: Cut a triangle as fig. 1. Turn under long diagonal edge and pin around head as illustrated: draw in neatly at back and catch ends together securely, then catch front edge to hair to hold in place.

EYES: Cut away lower third of sequin, as shown, and stitch into position. Alternatively, cut in felt or embroider.

CRYSTAL BALL: Stick or pin (or both) to fix against body: then bend hands round to hold it, as illustrated.

Father Francis, the jovial friar

Blessings flow from the benign features of this serenely happy friar. Not least of which is the fact that he's so quick and easy to make.

MATERIALS: Flesh felt for head, body, hands and feet: 20×15 cm (8×6 in)
Mid-brown felt for habit: 30 cm (12 in) square
Dark brown felt for skull cap and sandals: 8 cm (3 in) square
Scrap of black felt for eyes
Thick brown yarn or fine cord for belt
Medium-weight knitting wool or yarn for hair
Black sewing thread for features
Stranded embroidery cotton for mouth
18 cm (7 in) string of small wooden beads

BASIC DOLL: Follow the directions (p. 44) for Body B—*with a shorter neck*, and make the feet in flesh felt.

SANDALS: Cut the upper and sole twice each in dark brown. Wrap the upper over the top of the foot, and catch (or stick) side edges underneath. Stick sandal sole securely to sole of foot.

HABIT: Cut the bodice and cowl once each: cut a piece 13×23 cm (5×9 in) for the skirt.

Join sleeve and side seams A–B–C. Join cowl to bodice around neck edge, right side of cowl to wrong side of bodice.

Join short side edges of skirt to form centre back seam. Gather top edge,

FATHER FRANCIS
Actual size

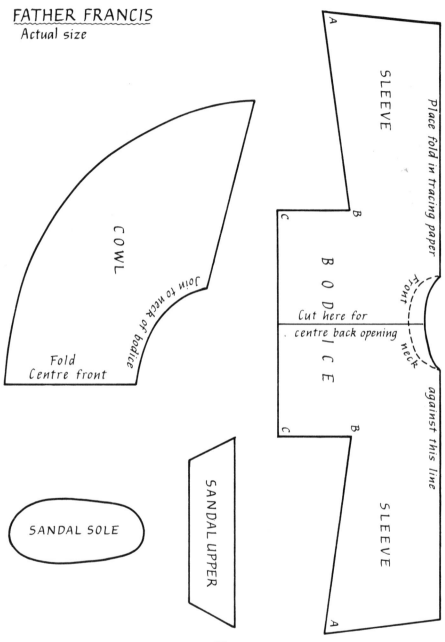

SLEEVE

Place fold in tracing paper

COWL

Join to neck of bodice

BODICE

Cut here for
centre back opening

front

neck

against this line

Fold
Centre front

SLEEVE

SANDAL UPPER

SANDAL SOLE

marking centre front and sides. Right sides together, pin skirt to lower edge of bodice, distributing gathers evenly: stitch securely. Turn to right side and gather lower edge of bodice.

Fit on doll and slip-stitch centre back opening. Draw up gathers around waist and catch to body. Right sides together, join straight edges of cowl.

Tie belt around waist, looping beads through as illustrated.

HAIR: Use a strip of stiff (or folded) paper—or thin card—2 cm ($\frac{3}{4}$ in) deep by about 30 cm (12 in) long. Wind the wool or yarn very evenly around the paper, pushing the strands closely together. Using matching thread, backstitch along the top edge, taking up a few strands at a time—but making sure you don't miss any. When you have covered 18–20 cm (7–8 in), cut the loops along the lower edge, and remove the paper carefully, to prevent twisting. Stick or stitch around head, as illustrated: trim neatly (slightly shorter across forehead), and stick strands down if necessary.

SKULL CAP: Cut a 4 cm (1$\frac{1}{2}$ in) diameter circle of felt. Gather very close to the edge, then draw up to fit top of head and stick into place.

FEATURES: Cut (or punch) 5 mm ($\frac{3}{16}$ in) diameter circles of black felt for eyes, and stick or sew into position. Embroider the mouth in outline or stem stitch, using two strands of cotton. The eyebrows and nose are straight stitches, using double and single sewing thread, respectively.

Dingleweed, the lucky gnome

He's such a friendly little creature, with his fluffy white baby-knit whiskers! Cutting him down to size is just a simple matter of shortening the arms and legs of the basic doll.

MATERIALS: Flesh felt for head, body and hands: 15 cm (6 in) square
Red felt for jersey and cap: 20 cm (8 in) square
Green felt for jerkin: 14 × 7 cm (5$\frac{1}{2}$ × 2$\frac{3}{4}$ in)
Gold felt for trousers: 10 × 15 cm (4 × 6 in)
Dark brown felt for boots: 15 × 10 cm (6 × 4 in)
Mid- (or dark) brown felt for soles: 5 cm (2 in) square
14 cm (5$\frac{1}{2}$ in) brown felt, ribbon or braid, 1 cm ($\frac{3}{8}$ in) wide, for belt
6 cm (2$\frac{1}{2}$ in) very narrow braid for buckle

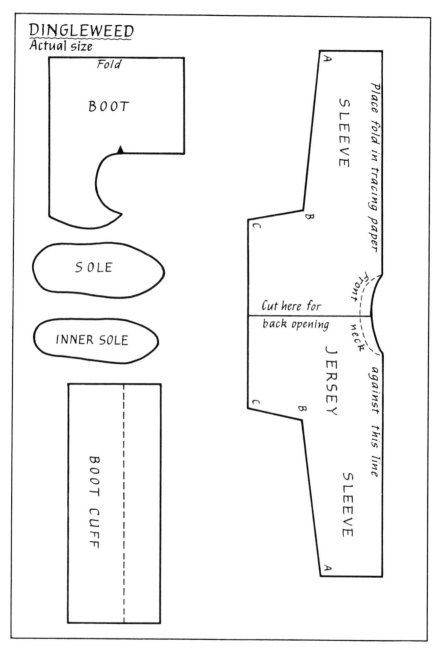

DINGLEWEED
Actual size

Fold

BOOT

SOLE

INNER SOLE

BOOT CUFF

A

SLEEVE

B

C

Place fold in tracing paper

front

Cut here for
back opening

neck

JERSEY

C

B

against this line

SLEEVE

A

2 black sequins for eyes, about 7 mm (¼ in) diameter (optional)
Small pink bead for nose
Fluffy white knitting wool or yarn for hair
Small bell, and a pipe cleaner (optional), for cap

BASIC DOLL: Follow the directions (p. 44) for Body B, *with a shorter neck*. Shorten the limbs as follows: cut the arm foam 3 × 17 cm (1¼ × 6½ in)—and cut the pipe cleaners and foam each 2 cm (¾ in) shorter for the legs. Substitute boot patterns for foot and sole (see below).

TROUSERS: See basic directions (p. 52).

JERSEY: Cut in felt (cut cap at the same time). Join sleeve and side seams A–B–C, and turn to right side. Fit on doll and pin into position: slip-stitch centre back opening.

JERKIN: Cut in felt. Join side seams A–B, and turn to right side. Fit on doll and slip-stitch centre back opening.
Stick belt around waist, and stick braid at centre front for buckle, as illustrated.

BOOTS: Cut boot, cuff and sole in appropriate felts, and the inner sole in card. Then make up and fit boot as directed on p. 50 (trouser leg inside). Fold top edge of cuff under, as broken line, and stick around top of boot, oversewing join at back.

CAP: Join straight edges to form centre back seam, and turn to right side. Fit pipe cleaner up into point, and catch to felt at base of seam: cut off surplus. Stitch bell to tip.

FEATURES: Stitch bead into position for nose. Cut away lower section of sequins and stitch to face, as illustrated. Alternatively, cut in felt or embroider.

BEARD AND HAIR: Prepare a strip of stiff (or folded) paper—or thin card—2 cm (¾ in) deep by about 20 cm (8 in) long. Wind the wool or yarn very evenly around the paper, pushing the strands closely together. Using matching thread, back-stitch along one edge, taking up a few strands at a time but

61

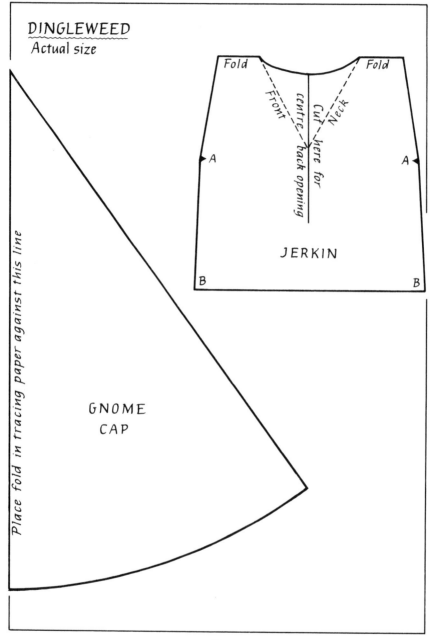

DINGLEWEED
Actual size

Fold   Fold

Front
centre - back opening
Cut here for
Neck

A   A

B   B

JERKIN

Place fold in tracing paper against this line

GNOME
CAP

making sure you don't miss any. Now push the loops off the strip very carefully, to prevent twisting.

Pin the looped fringe around the face and back of head—also pinning the cap into place to determine correct positioning. When satisfied, stick beard, hair and finally, the cap, to head—adding a tuft of loops at centre front, to emerge below edge of cap.

Children of Yesterday and Today

Nostalgic memories

———————◆••◆———————

Just fun to have around: these dolls make good companions for any age. Each has an individual charm that guarantees sales-appeal.

Nanny Toogood and the Twins

The very best nannies wear long, red flannel pantaloons as a Sensible Precaution. But both these and the petticoat can be omitted to save time and materials. The babies are very simple: nevertheless, they *are* an additional item—which must be reflected in the selling price. However, the tiny pair double the charm of the subject, so customers will be getting full value for money.

MATERIALS:
Flesh felt for head, body and hands: 15 cm (6 in) square
Black felt for boots: 9 × 8 cm (3½ × 3 in)
Brown (or black) felt for soles: 4 cm (1½ in) square
Red felt for pantaloons: 11 × 15 cm (4½ × 6 in)
Dark blue felt for dress: 23 cm (9 in) square
White felt for apron and cap: 12 × 10 cm (5 × 4 in)
Vilene or Pellon for petticoat: 11 × 20 cm (4¼ × 8 in)
18 cm (7 in) narrow heavy white lace for collar and cuffs
20 cm (8 in) white ribbon, about 1 cm (⅜ in) wide—plus lace—to trim cap
2 small sequins for eyes (optional)
Black sewing thread for features
Stranded embroidery cotton for mouth
Medium-weight knitting wool or yarn for hair

For *each* baby:

Papier mâché, pressed cotton, wood, or alternative ball, 2.5 cm (1 in) in diameter, for head (or use Harbutt's Plasticine or Plastone)

64

Cowboy Larry and Jamie, the winter sports enthusiast

Father Francis, the jovial friar and Gipsy Crystal Rose

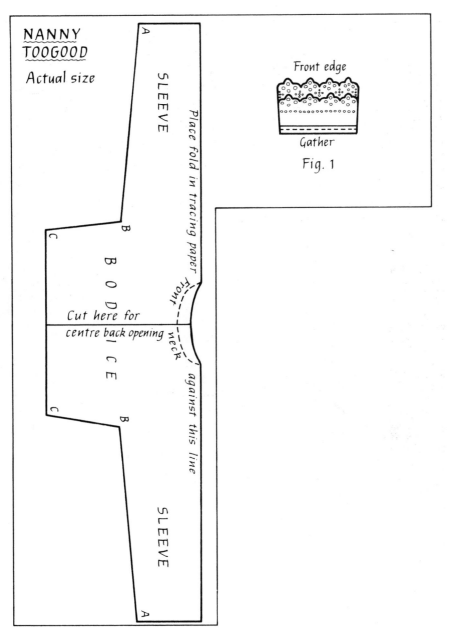

NANNY
TOOGOOD

Actual size

SLEEVE

Place fold in tracing paper

A

B

C

BODICE

Cut here for
centre back opening

Front neck

against this line

C

B

SLEEVE

A

Front edge

Gather

Fig. 1

65

Flesh poster colour to paint head, if necessary
8 cm ($3\frac{1}{4}$ in) pipe cleaner
Sheet foam, 1 cm ($\frac{3}{8}$ in) thick (or wadding/cotton batting), for body: 4×5 cm ($1\frac{1}{2} \times 2$ in)
White felt for petticoat: 4.5×7 cm ($1\frac{3}{4} \times 2\frac{3}{4}$ in)
Cream fabric for dress: 7×10 cm ($2\frac{3}{4} \times 4$ in)
25 cm (10 in) cream lace, 2 cm ($\frac{3}{4}$ in) deep, for bonnet and hem
Pink or blue embroidery or lace trim for bonnet and dress
Scrap of knitting wool or yarn for hair
Felt pen or black ink for eyes

BASIC DOLL: Follow the directions (p. 44) for Body B—*with a shorter neck*: cut the whole foot in black, for boots.

PANTALOONS: Follow basic directions (p. 52), drawing up tightly around ankles.

PETTICOAT: As Gipsy Crystal Rose (p. 56).

DRESS: Cut the bodice once, and a piece 11.5×23 cm ($4\frac{1}{2} \times 9$ in) for the skirt.
Join sleeve and side seams A–B–C.
Join short side edges of skirt to form centre back seam. Gather top edge, marking centre front and sides. Right sides together, pin skirt to lower edge of bodice, distributing gathers evenly: stitch securely. Turn to right side and stitch lace around neck and wrists, as illustrated.
Fit on doll and slip-stitch centre back opening.

APRON: Cut white felt 9 cm ($3\frac{1}{2}$ in) deep $\times$ 8 cm ($3\frac{1}{4}$ in) wide, and a strip 1×12 cm ($\frac{3}{8} \times 5$ in) for the belt.
Gather top edge of apron and draw up across front of dress, catching to lower edge of bodice. Stick belt around waist, joining at back.

HAIR: Follow directions for Gipsy Crystal Rose (p. 56), adding a bun at nape of neck: wind wool or yarn about 10 times around the tips of three fingers, then twist, and catch the loops together neatly. Stick or sew into place.

FEATURES: Stitch sequins to face for eyes, or embroider with black thread, adding straight stitches for eyebrows. Embroider mouth in outline or stem stitch, using two strands of cotton.

CAP: Trim the edge and centre of a 4 cm (1½ in) diameter circle of felt with lace. Fold ribbon in half and stitch underneath back of cap to hang down as streamers: cut ends in an inverted V-shape.

Fix on top of head.

TO MAKE EACH BABY: Bend pipe cleaner in half and push bent end into ball. Paint ball, if necessary, and leave to dry.

BODY: Join shorter edges of foam to form centre back seam: slip cut ends of pipe cleaner inside, then bind top end of foam tightly with thread, under head.

PETTICOAT: Join short edges of felt to form centre back seam, and turn to right side. Gather top edge: fit over body and draw up tightly, close under head.

DRESS: Right side inside, join short edges of fabric to form centre back seam. Turn to right side and trim lower edge with lace. Turn top edge under and gather just below fold. Fit on doll and draw up tightly around neck. Trim front.

HAIR: Wind wool or yarn 3–4 times around a finger-tip, then bind centre tightly with matching thread and fix to head, as illustrated (or wait until fitting bonnet, to check position).

BONNET: Cut two 6 cm (2½ in) lengths of lace: place the front edge of one piece over the straight back edge of the other, and join (fig. 1). Then gather the back edge and draw up tightly to form back of bonnet. Fit on doll: gather cut edge, taking thread across front, under chin, and draw up around neck. Stick trimming at side.

EYES: Mark small dots with felt pen or black ink.

Bridesmaid Posy

If Posy is wondering why she's so often a bridesmaid . . . perhaps it's because she looks so enchanting with Nanny and the twins in the photograph. Crisp broderie anglaise or eyelet embroidery makes the prettiest of dresses: and it's not as extravagant as it looks, since nothing is wasted (you can adjust the

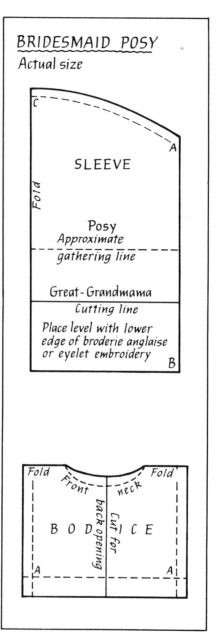

BRIDESMAID POSY
Actual size

SLEEVE

Fold

Posy
Approximate
gathering line

Great-Grandmama
Cutting line

Place level with lower
edge of broderie anglaise
or eyelet embroidery

C

A

B

Fold

Fold

Front **neck**

back opening

Cut for

B O D I C E

A

A

width of skirts and sleeves slightly to fall in with the embroidered design). But Posy can look just as charming in an ordinary fabric—a flowered cotton, perhaps: just allow extra for turning up hems, and trim with lace or an embroidered edging.

MATERIALS: Flesh felt for head, body, hands and feet: 20 × 15 cm (8 × 6 in)
Mid-brown felt for soles: 4 cm (1½ in) square
Scrap of black felt for eyes
60 cm (24 in) cream broderie anglaise or eyelet embroidery, 12 cm (4¾ in) deep, for dress (or alternative fabric)
Medium-weight soft Vilene or Pellon for petticoat and pantalettes: 11 × 30 cm (4½ × 12 in)
30 cm (12 in) blue lace, about 2 cm (¾ in) deep, to trim underwear
40 cm (15 in) cream lace, about 2 cm (¾ in) deep, for head-dress and bouquet
25 cm (¼ yd) embroidered flower trimming, or alternative, for head-dress and collar
40 cm (15 in) narrow blue ribbon for sash
20 cm (8 in) narrow cream braid (or ribbon) for shoes
8 cm (3 in) narrow green braid for bouquet
Tiny blue lace or other motifs to trim shoes
Tiny blue flowers for bouquet
2 small sequins for eyes (optional)
Medium-weight knitting wool or yarn for hair

BASIC DOLL: Make as directed (p. 44), with Body A: cut feet in flesh.

SHOES: Stick braid around foot, level with lower edge, beginning and ending at the front. Stick a tiny lace motif (e.g. half-a-daisy) or similar trim over join.

PANTALETTES: Follow basic directions (p. 52), trimming the ankles with blue lace.

PETTICOAT: Cut Vilene or Pellon 11 cm (4½ in) deep × 16 cm (6½ in) wide.
Join short edges to form centre back seam, and turn to right side. Stitch lace around lower edge. Gather top edge: mark centre front and sides, then fit on doll and draw up around waist, distributing gathers evenly. Catch into place.

UNDERSKIRT: Cutting in broderie anglaise or eyelet embroidery, make and fit exactly as petticoat (above).

OVERSKIRT: Cut 10 cm (4 in) deep × 20 cm (8 in) wide. Then make up and fit in the same way, but *above* natural waistline, drawing up gathers close under arms.

SLEEVES: Cut twice. Right side inside, join side edges A–B, and turn to right side. Gather top edge and fit sleeve on doll. Draw up gathers around top of arm, point C level with shoulder seam: distribute evenly and catch neatly over edge of body felt.

Gather sleeve about halfway down, and draw up tightly around arm.

BODICE: Cut once. Turn under side edges, as broken lines (tack or baste, if necessary), then turn up lower edges in the same way.

Fit on doll, pinning centre back opening so that cut edges meet: then slip-stitch together, taking up a little body felt too. Catch lower corners (A) of front and back loosely together under each arm, then catch side edges neatly over sleeve gathers, and lower edges over waist gathers.

COLLAR: Stick embroidery around neck, overlapping cut edge of bodice.

SASH: Tie ribbon around waistline, catching bow at centre back. Trim cut ends neatly.

HAIR: Prepare a strip of stiff (or folded) paper—or thin card—2.5 cm (1 in) deep by about 10 cm (4 in) wide. Wind the wool or yarn around the paper about 10 times, then catch the loops tightly together with matching thread, and slide off. Make a second bunch of loops in the same way.

Now follow the directions for *the first skein only* of Gipsy Crystal Rose's hair (p. 56). When this is in position, stitch a bunch of loops at each side of the head, over the seam and immediately below the end of the skein.

Continue and complete hairstyle as directed on p. 56.

To make her fringe, wind wool or yarn very evenly around the paper strip, pushing the strands closely together. Using matching thread, back-stitch along the top edge, taking up a few strands at a time—but making sure you don't miss any. When you have covered about 4 cm (1½ in), push the loops off the strip very carefully, to prevent twisting. Stick or sew the looped fringe in a curve, covering the front half of the head and overlapping the forehead.

Make a similar length of looped fringe and stitch across back of head, below ends of skeins.

EYES: See 'felt and sequin' method (p. 51), or alternative.

HEAD-DRESS: Gather straight edge of a 25 cm (10 in) length of lace: join cut ends and draw up to form a circle, the open centre about 2.5 cm (1 in) in diameter. Stick or sew trimming over inner gathered edge.
Fix securely to head.

BOUQUET: Gather braid in a circle, as lace for head-dress, but draw up tightly, close under flower-heads. Make a similar circle with about 12 cm (5 in) lace, and draw up tightly around stalks, immediately under braid.
Stitch stalks to palm of hand.

Alexander and Eliza-Kate

Looking as if they have just stepped from the pages of a favourite childhood storybook, Alexander and Eliza-Kate are a lovable pair of eight-year-olds from the 1800s. Obviously there's a little more work in this endearing couple—but they're still as simple to make as all the other dolls.

With minimal adaptation, the usual basic doll is scaled down to child-size proportions. For the girl's dress, try to find narrow braids which can be cut in half down the centre to make an even finer trimming (see photograph). Otherwise, use the narrowest braids available: quantities are given for both alternatives.

Alexander

MATERIALS: Flesh felt for head, body and hands: 15 cm (6 in) square
Mid-blue felt for knickerbockers: 8 × 15 cm (3¼ × 6 in)
Light (or mid-) blue felt for cap: 15 cm (6 in) diameter circle
Olive green felt for jacket: 10 × 13 cm (4 × 5¼ in) *plus* a strip 1.5 × 20 cm (⅝ × 8 in) for the cap band
Gold felt for waistcoat/vest: 4 × 6 cm (1¼ × 2¼ in)
White felt for shirt: 12 × 14 cm (5 × 5½ in)
Dark brown felt for cap and boots: 10 × 15 cm (4 × 6 in)
Mid-brown felt for stockings: 4 × 8 cm (1¾ × 3¼ in)

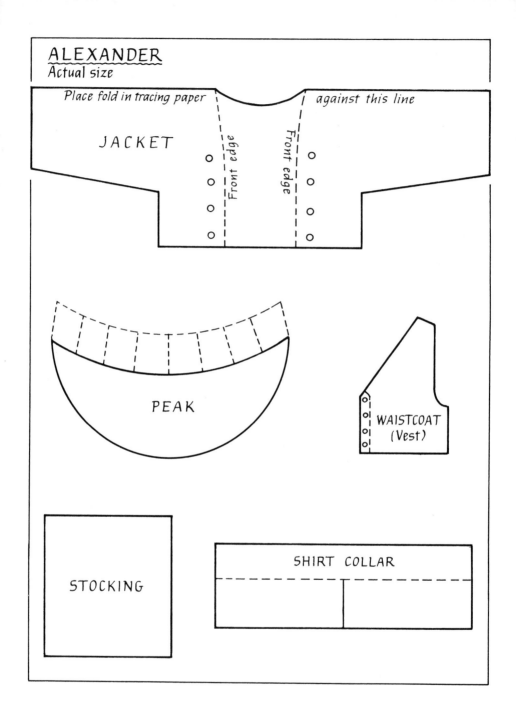

ALEXANDER
Actual size

Place fold in tracing paper | against this line

JACKET

Front edge

Front edge

PEAK

WAISTCOAT
(Vest)

STOCKING

SHIRT COLLAR

Brown felt for soles: 4 cm (1½ in) square
Scrap of black felt for eyes
8 cm (3 in) narrow black ribbon for bow-tie
16 cm (6 in) fine black crochet cotton, etc, for bootlaces
8 small gilt beads for jacket buttons
4 tiny black beads for waistcoat/vest buttons
2 small sequins for eyes (optional)
Medium-weight knitting wool or yarn for hair
Thin flexible card for cap
Face tissues (optional)

BASIC DOLL: Make as directed on p. 44, but adjust the measurements as follows. Trace a shorter body pattern, following lines A for *top* half (to waist), but *broken* lines for lower half.

Cut the body foam 9.5 × 4 cm (3¾ × 1½ in): cut the arm foam 3 × 17 cm (1¼ × 6½ in): cut the foam for each leg 10 × 4 cm (4 × 1½ in), and the leg pipe cleaners 14.5 cm (5¾ in).

Ignore the feet at this stage (see below).

SHIRT: Cut in white felt. Join sleeve and side seams A–B–D, and turn to right side. Fit on doll and pin centre back opening: then slip-stitch edges together.

KNICKERBOCKERS: Cut the basic trouser pattern (p. 53) twice, shortening as indicated. Cut the stocking twice, in brown.

Gather the lower edge of each trouser leg: then, right sides together, join the gathered edge of the trouser to the top edge of a stocking, drawing up to fit, and distributing the gathers evenly. Right side inside, join the side edges of each stocking.

Now complete as basic trouser directions (p. 49). Fit waist edge over shirt, and lower edges of stockings just above base of legs.

BOOTS: Shorten basic foot pattern (p. 48) as broken line: cut twice in dark brown, and then follow basic directions. Secure boot over stocking, then loop 8 cm (3 in) crochet cotton into a 'bow', and catch at centre front.

WAISTCOAT/VEST: Cut twice in felt. Overlap the centre front edges as broken line, and catch lightly together. Pin smoothly over shirt front, just overlapping top of knickerbockers, then slip-stitch shoulder and side edges neatly into place.

JACKET: Cut in green felt. Join sleeve and side seams and turn to right side. Fit on doll (note protruding cuffs of shirt).

COLLAR: Cut in white. Slit centre front, as indicated, then fold top section under as broken line. Fit around neck: trim ends and join neatly at back.

BOW-TIE: Fold cut ends of ribbon under to meet at centre, forming two loops. Catch together and stitch inside collar opening, close under chin, as illustrated.

HAIR: The method is exactly the same as the boy's hairstyle described on p. 29: but of course the proportions are different, and again you will have to experiment with the weight of wool or yarn you are using, to achieve the correct effect.

To adjust for these differences in Alexander's case, the wool was wound 10 times around a 5 cm (2 in) card for the two front bunches (at x): but only 8 times around the same card for the back bunches.

For the top section, the wool was wound 15 times around a 13 cm (5 in) deep card—and then a thread run through the strands 5 cm (2 in) above the lower edge.

All other directions, and the diagrams, are equally applicable, adapted as above.

EYES: See 'felt and sequin' method (p. 51)—or alternative.

CAP: Cut a strip of card 20 cm (8 in) long × 1.5 cm ($\frac{5}{8}$ in) deep. Cover one side with green felt: leave a tiny overlap of felt along one long edge, but trim remaining edges level. Fit band around head, and mark overlap.

Gather close to cut edge of light blue felt circle. Mark edge into quarters, and mark band into four. Then draw up gathers and, right sides together, oversew gathers to overlapping edge of band, distributing evenly between marked points. Turn carefully to right side: trim and stick overlapping band.

Cut peak in card (ignoring broken lines): cover one side with dark brown felt, trimming edges level. Now cover underside—but allow extra behind inner curve, as broken lines: cut surplus into tabs, as indicated. Fit inner curve of peak at front of cap, level with lower edge of band, and stick tabs neatly up inside.

Stick a small circle of green felt to crown for centre button.

Place one or two lightly crumpled tissues inside to hold in shape.

BUTTONS: Stick beads to jacket and waistcoat/vest, as illustrated.

Eliza-Kate

MATERIALS: Flesh felt for head, body and hands: 15 cm (6 in) square
Rose felt for dress: 20 cm (8 in) square
Caramel felt for cape and hat: 25 cm (10 in) square
Black felt for boots and eyes: 9 cm (3½ in) square
Brown (or black) felt for soles: 4 cm (1½ in) square
Medium-weight soft Vilene or Pellon: 7.5 × 18 cm
(3 × 7 in) for petticoat, and 8 × 15 cm (3¼ × 6 in) for pantalettes
30 cm (12 in) dark brown braid, about 1 cm (⅜ in) wide, for hem and cuffs
40 cm (16 in) narrow dark brown braid for skirt: if possible, cut a further 20 cm (8 in) of above braid in half
25 cm (10 in) caramel braid, about 1 cm (⅜ in) wide, for cape—*to be cut in half* (if not possible, substitute 50 cm (20 in) narrow braid)
40 cm (16 in) very narrow cream braid to edge hat brim
25 cm (9 in) pink velvet ribbon, 2 cm (¾ in) wide, for hatband
25 cm (9 in) pink lace daisies, or alternative, for inside brim
Tiny flower trim for waist (optional)
10 cm (4 in) very narrow white lace for cuffs
35 cm (13 in) white lace, about 2 cm (¾ in) deep, to trim petticoat and pantalettes
6 tiny black beads for boot buttons (optional)
2 small sequins for eyes (optional)
Medium-weight knitting wool or yarn for hair
Thin flexible card for hat

BASIC DOLL: As Alexander (p. 73)—but add feet, using black felt.

PANTALETTES: Follow basic directions (p. 52), trimming the ankles with lace.

PETTICOAT: Join short side edges to form centre back seam, and turn to right side. Stitch lace around hem. Gather top edge: mark centre front and sides, then fit on doll and draw up around waist, distributing gathers evenly. Catch into place.

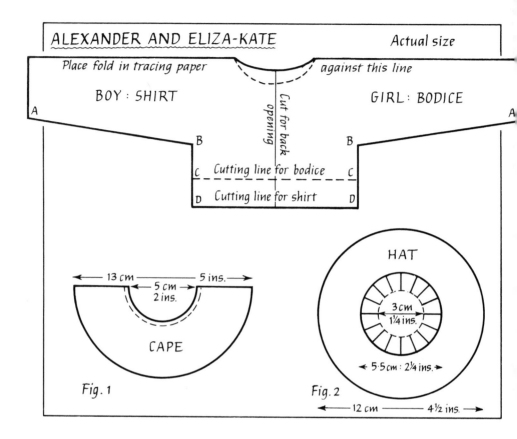

ALEXANDER AND ELIZA-KATE   Actual size

Place fold in tracing paper   *against this line*

BOY : SHIRT   GIRL : BODICE

A   A

Cut for back opening

B   B

C   Cutting line for bodice   C

D   Cutting line for shirt   D

13 cm — 5 ins.
5 cm
2 ins.

CAPE

HAT

3 cm
1¼ ins.

5·5 cm : 2¼ ins.

Fig. 1   Fig. 2

12 cm   4½ ins.

DRESS: Cut bodice once, and a piece 8.5 × 20 cm (3¼ × 8 in) for the skirt.
Join sleeve and side seams A–B–C.

Join short side edges of skirt to form centre back seam. Gather top edge, marking centre front and sides. Right sides together, pin skirt to lower edge of bodice, distributing gathers evenly: stitch securely. Turn to right side. Gather 5 cm (2 in) lace around each wrist, then stick or sew bands of braid around wrists and skirt, as illustrated. Stitch flower trim at waist.

Fit on doll and slip-stitch centre back opening.

CAPE: Cut as fig. 1. Trim front and lower edges with narrow (half-width) braid. Gather neck edge, as indicated: fit on doll, draw up, and join top corners at centre front. Wrap braid (full-width) around neck and join neatly, for collar, catching lower edge to cape.

HAIR: Cut about ten 18 cm (7 in) lengths of wool or yarn: stitch these to centre top of head, over seam, so that about 5 cm (2 in) overlaps forehead and remainder hangs down centre back of head.

Then follow the directions for the *first and second stages only* for Gipsy Crystal Rose's hair (p. 56).

Now wind wool about 15 times around the 13 cm (5 in) deep card: tie tightly at one edge, then cut along the other. Lift loose strands at back of head, and stitch tied centre of new piece underneath, to crown of head, directly behind first skein. Spread adhesive over back of head, then arrange strands smoothly so that the area is evenly covered, replacing original strands at centre. Catch at each side to ends of front skeins.

Trim cut ends across back, and neaten fringe.

EYES: See 'felt and sequin' method (p. 51)—or alternative.

HAT: Cut a 12 cm (4½ in) diameter circle of card for the brim, with a 5.5 cm (2¼ in) hole in the centre. Cover one side with felt, trimming edges level. Now cover under-side, but cut the inner circle only 3 cm (1¼ in) in diameter (fig. 2), snipping the surplus into tabs, as indicated.

Cut a strip of card 20 cm (8 in) long × 2.5 cm (1 in) deep, for the sides. Cover one side with felt: leave a tiny overlap of felt along the long top edge, but trim remaining edges level.

Cover a 5.5 cm (2¼ in) diameter circle of card with felt for the crown, leaving a tiny overlap, as before.

Oversew the top edge of the side around the crown, stitching the overlapping felt neatly. Trim and stick card overlap. Fit brim underneath, sticking tabs neatly up inside.

Fix velvet ribbon around sides. Stick narrow braid around outer edge of brim—and daisy trim, or alternative, underneath (as illustrated).

BOOT BUTTONS: Stick beads to sides of boots, as shown.

Packaging and Presentation

———◆◆◆◆◆———

First and foremost, your dolls need protection from the eager hands of prospective buyers! Combine this with an attractive form of presentation, and you will not only safeguard the doll, but also enhance its appearance.

Try to package the doll so that a potential purchaser can inspect is as fully as possible without unwrapping it—just in case they change their mind. There are several forms of clear wrapping materials from which to choose: have a look at your local stationer, department store or supermarket. See-through cooking or freezer film, is my favourite, because it is self-sealing: simply stretch the 'cling-film' over the merchandise, and overlap the edges.

A card backing, slightly larger than the figure, is often sufficient protection. Cut an oblong or oval shape from a cereal or similar carton, and paste coloured paper or gift-wrap over both sides—or use a lacy paper doily for an extra pretty background. Fix the doll in place with double-sided tape: then cover with film, taking all the edges smoothly round to overlap at the back.

Empty face-tissue cartons provide ideal boxes for smaller dolls—and make them look rather special, too. Cut off the top, then cover the outside with gift-wrap, folding doilies or tissue paper cut with pinking shears to overlap the top edge. Pack the doll in a bed of crumpled tissues, then cover with film as before.

A small doll can appear to 'stand up' for display purposes by setting it on a card base. Cut a rectangle or square to fit flat inside the bottom of a see-through bag: fold the corners neatly down to form flat triangles underneath, and fix with tape. Place the doll upright inside the bag, then draw the top edge together and tie with coloured string or ribbon.

And don't forget that final exclusive touch: a neat self-adhesive or tie-on label displaying your name—and that of the doll.

Where to Buy the Materials

All the items used were deliberately chosen because they should be easily obtainable, wherever you live. However, if you experience any difficulty—here are my own favourite sources of supply.

Coloured felts, wool and yarn, fancy braids and trimmings, lace, ribbon, beads, flowers, stuffing and other craft materials—and all sewing equipment:

> John Lewis
> Oxford Street, London W1A 1EX
> Peter Jones
> Sloane Square, London SW1W 8BL
> Craftsmith
> Exeter : Hemel Hempstead : Manchester : Nottingham :
> Richmond : Slough : Southend

General craft materials, including coloured felts and stuffing:

> Arts and Crafts
> 10 Byram Street, Huddersfield, Yorks. HD1 1DA

Graph paper, greaseproof and tissue paper, adhesives, artists' materials and all general stationery:

> W. H. Smith and Son Limited

Sheet foam:

> F. W. Woolworth and Company Limited

Recommended adhesives:
> Copydex do-it-yourself adhesive (for fabric, paper, etc.)
> Bostik Stik n'fix (for beads and similar non-porous surfaces)